Basic Math

Subtracting and Taking Away

Richard Leffingwell

Heinemann Library
Chicago, Illinois

Customer Service   888–454–2279
Visit our website at www.heinemannlibrary.com

Photo research by Erica Newbery
Designed by Joanna Hinton-Malivoire
Printed in China by South China Printing Company Limited

10 09 08 07 06
10 9 8 7 6 5 4 3 2 1

Library of Congress Cataloging-in-Publication Data
Leffingwell, Richard.
  Subtracting and taking away / Richard Leffingwell.
     p. cm. -- (Basic math)
  Includes index.
  ISBN 1-4034-8156-3 (library binding-hardcover) -- ISBN 1-4034-8161-X (pbk.)
  1. Subtraction--Juvenile literature. 2. Group theory--Juvenile literature. I. Title.
II. Series: Leffingwell, Richard. Basic math. III. Series.
  QA115.L45 2006
  513.2'12--dc22
                              2006005176

Acknowledgments
The author and publisher are grateful to the following for permission to reproduce copyright material: Alamy pp. **14**, **15**, **16**; Getty Images (Photodisc Red/Davies & Starr) pp. **5**, **6**, **7**, **8**; Harcourt Education Ltd (www.mmstudios.co.uk) pp. **4**, **9–12**, **17–22**, back cover

Cover photograph reproduced with permission of Photolibrary (Brand X/Burke Triolo) and Jupiter Images (FoodPix)

Every effort has been made to contact copyright holders of any material reproduced in this book. Any omissions will be rectified in subsequent printings if notice is given to the publisher.

Contents

What Is Subtracting?

Subtracting can help you find out how many things you have left.

Subtracting is useful in many ways.

Subtracting Shells

Pretend that you have 5 shells.

You take 2 shells and give them to a friend.

5 – 2 = ?

How many shells do you have now?

Take away 2 shells from the group of 5.

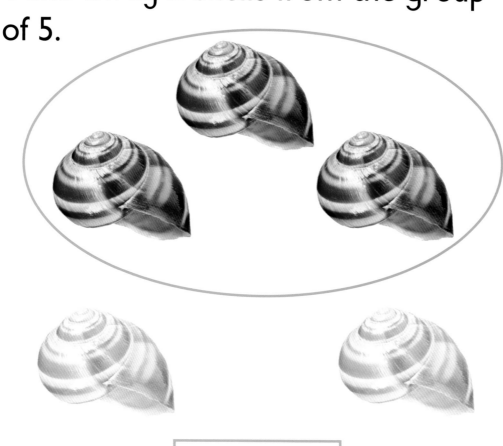

$$5 - 2 = 3$$

Now count to see how many you have left.

There are 3 left.

When you take away items from a group, you are subtracting them.

Subtracting Stones

$$6 - 2 = ?$$

Pretend that you have 6 stones and give 2 of them away.

How can you find out how many are left?

You can draw a picture and count the stones.

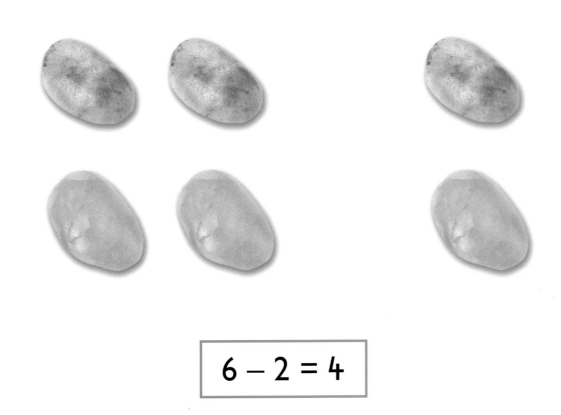

$$6 - 2 = 4$$

You have 4 left.

How else can you find out how many are left?

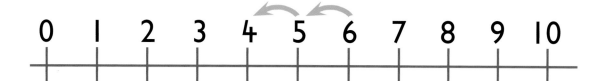

You can count back.

Count back once for each stone that was taken away.

Start counting back from 6.

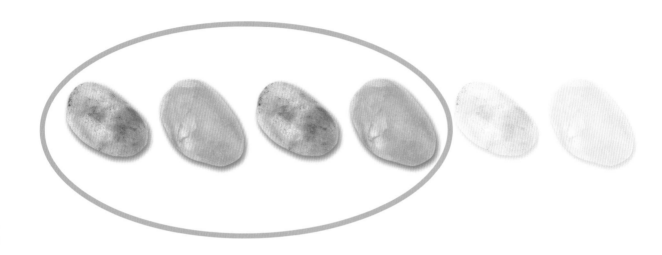

$$6 - 2 = 4$$

You took away 2 stones.

You have 4 stones left.

1   2   3   4   5   6

$$6 - 2 = 4$$

Counting back is when you count backwards from the number you started with.

You count back once for each thing that is taken away.

Subtracting Leaves

Pretend that you have 4 leaves and give 1 away.

Find out how many leaves you have by counting back.

You started with 4 leaves.

Count back from 4.

Count back 1 time.

Count back for each leaf that is taken away.

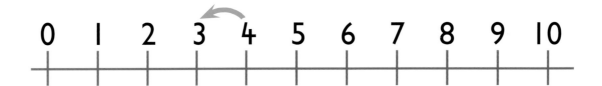

You counted back 1 time.

You have 3 leaves left.

Comparing Groups

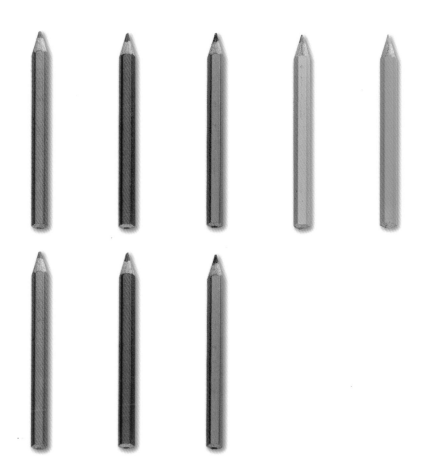

Pretend that you have 5 pencils.

Your friend has 3 pencils.

How many more pencils do you have?

To solve the problem, compare the two groups.

When you compare two groups, you are subtracting.

Look at the two groups.

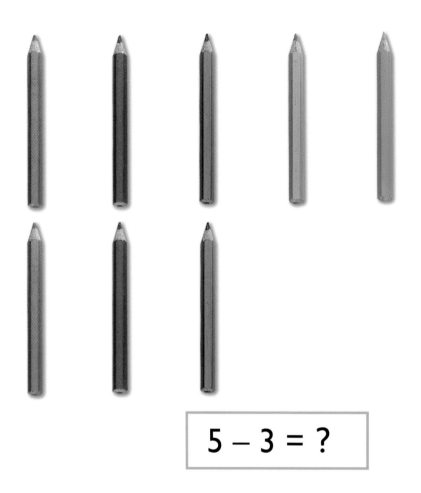

5 − 3 = ?

Can you see how many more pencils there are in your group?

You can see that 5 is 2 more than 3.

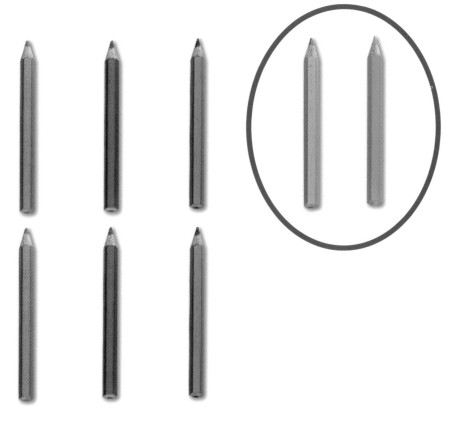

$$5 - 3 = 2$$

You have 2 more pencils.

Subtraction helps you find out how many of something is left.

$$8 - 2 = ?$$

You also subtract when you compare two groups.

You can find out how many more there are in the bigger group.

$$3 - 1 = ?$$

Quiz

Can you work out how many more red pencils there are?

Hint: Use the number line to count back.

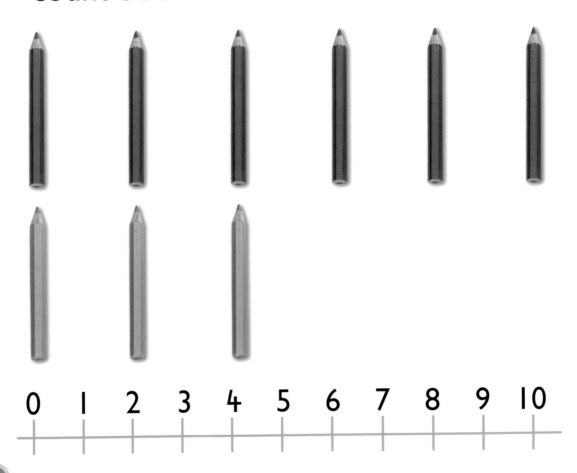

0   1   2   3   4   5   6   7   8   9   10

The Minus Sign

─ You use this sign to show that you are taking one number away from another.

$$3 - 2$$

When you take 2 away from 3, you get 1.

= You use the equals sign to show what 3 minus 2 is equal to.

$$3 - 2 = 1$$

Index

Answer to the quiz on page 22
There are 3 more red pencils.

Note to parents and teachers
Reading nonfiction texts for information is an important part of a child's literacy development. Readers can be encouraged to ask simple questions and then use the text to find the answers. Most chapters in this book begin with a question. Read the questions together. Look at the pictures. Talk about what the answer might be. Then read the text to find out if your predictions were correct. To develop readers' enquiry skills, encourage them to think of other questions they might ask about the topic. Discuss where you could find the answers. Assist children in using the contents page, picture glossary, and index to practice research skills and new vocabulary.